better together*

*This book is best read together, grownup and kid.

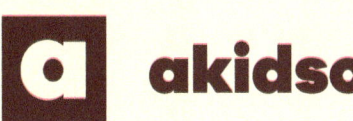 akidsco.com

a kids book about PLAY

by G Cody QJ Goldberg
in partnership with Harper's Playground

a kids book about

Text and design copyright © 2024
by A Kids Book About, Inc.

Copyright is good! It ensures that work like this can exist, and more work in the future can be created.

All rights reserved. No part of this publication may be reproduced, distributed, or transmitted in any form or by any means, including photocopying, recording, other electronic or mechanical methods, without the prior written permission of the publisher, except in the case of brief quotations embodied in critical reviews and certain other noncommercial uses permitted by copyright law. For permission requests, write to the publisher.

A Kids Book About, Kids Are Ready, and the colophon 'a' are trademarks of A Kids Book About, Inc.

Printed in the United States of America.

A Kids Book About books are available online: *akidsco.com*

To share your stories, ask questions, or inquire about bulk purchases (schools, libraries, and nonprofits), please use the following email address: *hello@akidsco.com*

Print ISBN: 979-8-89281-046-3
Ebook ISBN: 979-8-89281-047-0

Designed by Jelani Memory
Edited by Emma Wolf

Dedicated to my original playmates:
Beckers, DY, Buck, and Johnny,
and to my current playmates:
April, Harper, and Lennon.

And to my mom and dad, who
always encouraged me to play.

Intro

Hello! My name is Garfield Cody Quentin Jeffrey Goldberg. That's right, I have 5 names. I used to hide my name from people, but now that I'm older, I feel proud of it. I think my parents made my name kind of funny because they hoped I'd always remember to be playful.

Play is the way! Play is instinctive and essential and it is also unique to each individual. It is almost impossible to define, too. Play is most certainly the key ingredient to everything in the world that is good.

Play is also under attack. Kids are not getting nearly enough of it, and the negative impacts of that decline are showing far too often. My hope with this book is to encourage a continued love of play, and instill that love at as early of an age as possible! Growing up and leaving play behind just cannot be the status quo.

Let's protect play! It's really that important.

What is **play**?

Really, what do *you* think it is?

Right away, why don't you grab a piece of paper and write down some ideas, or talk about it with your grownup!

Now that you've had some time to think, can I tell you what I believe about play?

There are so many good
things that come from play.

Science. Art. Music. Engineering. Design. Sports.

All of these things require play to exist.

However, play is something that's super hard to define.

A lot of people try (scientists have been studying "play" for years), and no one totally agrees on what play is!

To me, I think of 2 main aspects
of play that really make it special:

1. Play is the universe's way of showing us it can be fun and rewarding to overcome our fears.

2. Play is how we find out what is most magical about ourselves.

OK, so what does all of that mean?

All of us have fears—it's
a totally human thing.

Part of overcoming challenges
involves tumbling, falling down,
getting back up, and trying again.

And guess what?
Play teaches us how to do this.

As kids, we engage physically
with things that might seem scary.

Climbing a rock, or a tree, riding a bike, balancing on a beam, performing on a stage—these are all **BIG** things.

But you know that feeling you get when you swing super high, or feel steady riding your bike, or hear the applause when you finish a performance?

Success.
Happiness.
Pure enjoyment!

It feels good to overcome new challenges, and it's extra good for our brain too.

To live in play is to live on the edge of fear and use that experience as motivation to move forward.

Through play we learn about all the amazing abilities we have.

Strength, flexibility, balance, responsiveness, agility, coordination, speed, and so much more.

These are lots of ways our physical bodies are magic in how they do what they do.

In play, we explore that beauty, and we also discover what's *unique* about us.

(Yes, that means you!)

What are your unique ideas?

What opinions do you have?

What can your body do?

What makes you feel happy, accomplished, at peace?

Through play and self-discovery, we can grow in confidence in who we are.

Accept who we are.

Love who we are and how our bodies work.

And when we accept and love ourselves, it's a natural next step to extend that to everyone else; this is called

EMPATHY!

Play gives us so much!

Now, kids, you're probably thinking...

"**No, DUH!*** I know all of this!
I was born to play!"

*That's something we used to say when I was a kid.

And you know what? I believe it.

Kids are so good at play.

I just really want to make sure you never forget it.

Grownups (like myself) can have a harder and harder time prioritizing play.

I know, right?!

It's such a bummer.

So, this book is to celebrate your love for play, and to encourage the grownups in your life to remember how much it matters.

You know what?

Why don't you put down this book right now and go play!

USLY!

Play your favorite game, explore the universe, maybe go outside and get some fresh air!

Oh, hey...you're still here?

You must be pretty good at play already!

Well, while we're taking a little break from playing, I've got something else to show you...

This drawing from my daughter, Lennon! Pretty cool, right?

In fact, maybe you'd like to make your own drawing. I hope you still have that piece of paper handy!

OK, OK, I do have some more stuff to share with you. So let's continue!

What do you think the rules of play are? I think about this a lot.

Are there any?

When I think of rules for play, it's not about what kind of things count as play (because everything can be play!).

It's more about how play should feel when you're a part of it.

So, how do these sound?

Rule #1:
Honesty.

When people are dishonest, that isn't fun, right?

I remember playing games with my friends when we all decided that cheating was actually part of the game, and that was fun.

BUT, if someone cheats when it's not part of the game, it's not really fun at all.

Rule #2:
Being nice.

There is no room for being mean when it comes to play.

It just doesn't feel right!

Play should be fun, it should make you laugh, it should make you feel closer to other people.

Meanness creates division— being nice brings us together.

A more playful world is a more peaceful world.

Rule #3:
Inclusion.
(This is a BIG one.)

No one should be excluded from play.

Play is for all of us, and we each belong at the heart of playing.

Everyone should be treated equally, everyone should be given a turn, and everyone should be valued for what they uniquely contribute.

And this is coming from
someone SUPER competitive.

But play isn't about competition.

It's inclusive.
It's collaborative.
It's magical.

Thanks for sticking
with me to the end.

We are definitely getting close to the last page, so...

Outro

Play creates connections in our brains and it teaches us that learning new skills is fun. Each new skill we learn makes playing that much more fun. And play also helps us discover what's cool and special about ourselves and those around us. Basically, play is a pretty big deal!

The goal of this book is to elevate the role of play every day and in everyone's lives. Why? A better future depends on it! So, spend time outside, make up new games, color, play dress-up, kick a ball around, wiggle your ears, tell jokes with your friends—SO many good and wonderful things in life are here because of play!

So, how do you want to play?

About The Author

G Cody QJ Goldberg (he/him) is a dreamer and he loves to play. He grew up playing outside, mostly in the rolling hills of Marin County, California. He quit an accidental 14-year corporate career to launch a nonprofit dedicated to making play inclusive for everyone. His family led a movement that designed, funded, and built the first totally inclusive playground in Portland, Oregon. Their passion project, Harper's Playground, was featured on NBC's The TODAY Show, and their family had a day named for them by the mayor of Portland for their efforts. **All of the proceeds of this book will be donated to Harper's Playground.**

Cody, his partner, April, their daughters, Harper and Lennon, and their dog, Millie, make their home in the beautiful Pacific Northwest.

 @harpersplayground    @harpersplayground

 harpersplayground.org

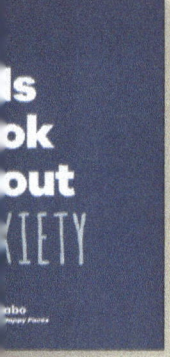

Discover more at akidsco.com

www.ingramcontent.com/pod-product-compliance
Lightning Source LLC
Chambersburg PA
CBHW061359010526
44107CB00012B/991